Big-Eyed Afraid

Big-Eyed Afraid

Erica Dawson

Foreword by

Mary Jo Salter

WAYWISER

First published in 2007 by

THE WAYWISER PRESS

14 Lyncroft Gardens, Ewell, Surrey KT17 1UR, UK
P.O. Box 6205, Baltimore, MD 21206, USA
www.waywiser-press.com

Managing Editor
Philip Hoy

Associate Editors
Joseph Harrison   Clive Watkins   Greg Williamson

A CIP catalogue record for this book is available from the British Library

ISBN-10: 1-904130-26-7   ISBN-13: 978-1-904130-26-0

Printed and bound by
Ingram / Lightning Source

For Mom, Dad, and Frank

Acknowledgements

The author wishes to thank the editors of the following journals in whose pages these poems first appeared (some under different titles): *Barrow Strreet*: "Motherland" and "Semantics"; *Blackbird*: "OCD" and "Placebo"; *Sewanee Theological Review*: "Coda," "Exam Room Three" and "Parallax"; *Southwest Review*: "Disorder"; *Virginia Quarterly Review*: "God Girl."

"Disorder" was first published in *Living in Storms: Contemporary Poetry and the Moods of Manic Depression*, edited by Thomas Schramm (Eastern Washington University Press, 2007).

Contents

Contents

Foreword by Mary Jo Salter

"I was born, Mom says…" is the refrain that opens the first and many other poems in this witty and distinctive debut collection. Erica Dawson's phrase is not David Copperfield's "I am born," but "I was born" – a reported event, since none of us remembers our first days. We readers pick up at once that this poet whose mother is "Mom" is young and clownish and a whiz-kid with diction:

> I was born, Mom says, Afro-
> Ready, a doll with woman's hair,
> Born eight-ball bald between two bare
> Legs now long grown, and, Oh
>
> Baby …

We're off and running now, in a speedy, playful whirlwind of a book. By its fourth line we know we're in the hands of a highly capable rhyme-and-meter maid, and have noted how skillfully Dawson manipulates word-order. We've inferred, that is, both that her legs are long and that she reached her adult height long ago. (She was born in 1979: not so long ago to some of us. Could this remarkable poet be only 28?)

We're going to hear a lot about Mom's appraisal of her talent-ed, musical baby, beautiful from head to toe. (Yes, we even get a poem, "High Heel," about the poet's shoes: "I'm patent, polished, buffed,/ Strap-bound and muled. I'm powder-puffed.") Dawson doesn't apologize for her own way of being female: "That's it," she says plainly. "I'm feminine." For all her straight talk, her sensual-ity is also tinged with wit – most amusingly in this parenthesis: "(conquered, I came)." But lest we imagine that her contemporary Song of Myself is going to be all celebration, all gaiety, many of the poems envision the poet's death. Reported birth, projected death: Dawson's body is forever having in-and-out-of-body experiences, and the distance she achieves from herself is what saves her poems from anything like navel-gazing. Profane, self-doubting, confes sional (especially in the zany and sad tour de force, "DrugFace," that concludes the collection), this poet is "big-eyed afraid," but not afraid to say so.

If Dawson reminds us in her headlong, enthralled narcissism of Whitman, she may call up even more the staccato verve, and the haunting obsessions, of Plath. In her fractured, then reassembled syntax, and in her pet names for her alter egos, she's got a bit of Berryman, too. James Merrill makes some appearances – in her punning, her obliquity, and her inventiveness in a poem like "Pianist pretending Chopin," a sonnet of two seven-line stanzas, whose rhymes match each other like her hands in the "mirrored Steinway." Sometimes the rules of Dawson's games, and her aplomb in winning them, are so preposterous that one can only laugh aloud. Anyone who has tried to write a sestina, in which six chosen end-words must keep reappearing in a rigidly prescribed order (but how to remember it? and why bother?), will surely marvel at Dawson's easy-but-way-too-hard solution. "In Consonance with the Order of Things" arranges that all 39 of its lines will end with the same word: "off." Even the line that seems to cheat, by concluding with "key of F," is on second glance perfectly correct. "Off" rhyme indeed!

Anthony Hecht was, among other accomplishments, a master of the sestina: he gave us one of the funniest in the language, "Sestina d'Inverno," and surely the most tragic, "The Book of Yolek." I believe he would have been delighted to see Erica Dawson, the second annual winner of the Anthony Hecht Poetry Prize, stepping up to the challenge. She owes much to her predecessors. And yet, already, there is nobody quite like her. That is saying a great deal.

I am a little world made cunningly
of elements ...

– John Donne

I

Nappyhead

I was born, Mom says, Afro-
Ready, a doll with woman's hair,
Born eight-ball bald between two bare
Legs now long grown, and, Oh

Baby, born with an infant's beard,
Lanugo blonde on tan – so fine
And Foxy Brown circa 1979
In a christening gown. Head smeared

With Lustrasilk, I wore
Six black-girl ponytails, barrettes
In geo-shapes and the alphabet's
Small caps, head dressed and more

Power to me. Parts
Curved with the scalp ran left and right
In a twice-crossed crucifix. At night,
The braids went loose. For tart's

Sake, I went red, called it
An accident then dyed my eye-
Brows too. I said I'd prettify
My lashes, benefit

From the cheap mascara wand
In purple-pink with fake strands glued
To mine – blue streaks, new attitude,
And eighties' chic *beau monde*.

If I cut more than a few
Short strands, Mom saved them in a bag
As a memento. Last year's shag
Smelled sweet with grease and shampoo,

And dried like paper, dead
Confetti kept in an envelope
With blood-stained baby teeth, jump rope,
And a sailor dress. I said

I'd make a wig – bouffant,
Bardot, big bang, and, man, that James
Brown pageboy's fly, man, *fly!* The dame's
Chignon- or debutante-

French twist – I've been the priss
Plucked hard, hot-waxed until the skin
Bubbles, straightened before the thin
Locks break beneath the hiss

And curling iron's steam.
I'm bleached, but call me Nappyhead,
And know that one week after I'm dead
The roots still grow, shea cream

And pomade gone, the bare
Legs freckled with follicles, the shaved-clean
Pussy's five-o'clock shadow, the Queen
Bee, now not worth a hair.

Doll Baby

I was born, Mom says, by the Slice-
N-Tug, Cesarean, just hand-
Picked like a toy from a trunk – God-tanned
And yet, *transparent?* ice-

Blue cord choking a hold
Around my neck. I convalesced
In incubator sheen, undressed
And darling, I've been told.

From preemie small, I grew
Past grown ("Goddamn Incredible Hulk.")
I'm too-short pants and breasts, all bulk,
And nipple peek-a-boo,

Barbie, and Glamour Do.
I'm Elegance. I've seen mom's scar,
And *my* stretch mark of *rouge et noir*,
The pubescent residue

From the navel down, from where
I grew – my pigment's treasure trail
Like bristle on an alpha male.
But am I debonair

Since someone told me once,
"You're big enough to be a man" –
Adam in Eve, all Dapper Dan
And Dressy Bessy? Once,

Twice, three times a lady? Yes,
Me tall? Yes. Model-like I'll lie
In a Da Vinci sprawl (*fee fi ...*)
And feminine finesse.

Doll Baby

I'm Stretch. I'm doll-like seams
Inside and out. My brain's in two
Halves split again. *In transitu*
My veins shoot blood in beams

Of brilliant red, the red
Of airbrushed lips, of toy-faced cheeks.
I'll flirt in flush because Clinique's
On sale. I'll lie in bed

Made-up, a daydream death
With playtime *rigor mortis*, id stiff
In still-life poise, and watch my midriff
Rise, and hear one last breath.

Post mortem, Mommy's prize
Will close her eyes and (finally) abstain,
The Porcelain Princéss, the Chatelaine
Dwindling to average size.

Mommy Dearest

Science says I was born to pro-
Create. Assume the alias
That forever in the daily is
Mommy. Nature says to grow

Babies conceived in-dish
Or -utero. Survival of
The fit? Fit them in vans where dove
Christs dive near Darwin fish.

That's it. I'm feminine.
I lie here somewhere in between
You're a woman now, the hymen's screen,
And fuck, the crying sin

Of a bastard boy, or, girl
Born after *Till Death* gold. My breasts
Roll to the side like palimpsests
Of puberty – a girl

Done good, I'm told. I've tensed
At the speculum's slick push. Latex
Reeked of birthday balloons, and the circumflex
Pussy, in accidents,

Puffed air, breathing Lamaze-
Birth breaths. At birth, I would've died
If midwives, fire-lit, had pried
Me loose to *oohs* and *ahs*,

To *Oh my Gods* while a pot
Boiled and mid-November burned
In frost. I would be buried, *urned*
In another time, begot

By God to a child-size box.
And yet tonight, able to ease
Out several possibilities
For junior me(s), for flocks

Of a Dawson kind called *Legs*
Or *Christ-What-A-Mess*, I'm birthing blood
As Mommy Dearest's girly stud,
Uddered and breeding eggs.

God Girl

I was born (*again?!*) two times:
Christened, then second dipped in a luke-
Warm pool with *Satan, I rebuke*
Thee, saved with pantomimes

(Hand down, across) and breath
Held with the Holy Ghost before
The family and the flock. Once more,
Bear me again. In death,

I'm good. At church, the hat
Appeared as a centerpiece of lace-
Wrapped buds. I watched the angel face
Stained in the ziggurat-

Like tiers of storied glass
Go flush in the sun, turn corpse-opaque
With clouds. And I, for heaven's sake,
Took heaven's biomass,

Washing feet first in the church-
White basement, hosed and pedicured.
I held the shot-glassed blood and stirred
Beside the Eden birch

Weeping to baked-in grass,
Green as a crayon. My fingertip
Went plum. Mom: *God, girl, take a sip*
Already. The church, en masse:

Amen. Good Lord. God Girl.
I love that end to the final verse,
Revelation to Genesis, Eve's curse
In blood, the sidewalk twirl

Of sisters in Gunne Sax
Chiffon, Ham's myth, and that dark dream
Where lepers lose their limbs, each ream
Of Bible type in black,

The Jesus red, the cracks
In the varnished pew, but most, the knell –
Less bleak than Longfellow's wailing bell
And forlorn amphibrachs,

But chimes the same for death,
I Do, or simply Sunday mass.
That bell, reverberating glass,
Is like an isopleth

Connecting day to day,
Ringing it New. And when the hearse
Carries me home, recite this verse,
This is my body. And say

I'm sacrilege in my
Best dress, God bless, and off to Hell
For that I shalt not ever tell.
Remember me as I

Go under, over, pass
And turn to Old, from God's Sweet Pea
Thrice born, in bone twice souled, to three
In liquid, solid, gas.

La Temptressa

When you whispered that, I said I was born to be
Your Eve, your apple, and your fatal femme.
Adore your Mephistopheles, Sweet Boy –
You've sold your soul. You leaned on the vanity
And, gawking, watched me in the bath. I thought
Love poems, pillaging epigraphs – *O Man's
First disobedience and this one, yours.*

(And if I scored a love poem, I'd invoke
Fair Aphrodite, say fuck off, then kill
Her dove-white swan because I'm prettier.
Calliope would write our story in
Our own reflections on the steamy mirror.
The words would form and drop just like a tear.

Young, black, and, Boy, would I be beautiful.

I'd sip on dry champagne and lick my lips.
I'd burst the bubble on my hip and make
A heart from a single strand of brown hair clinging
To the tile. The heart would drip. You'd watch
Me tease with a dangling leg and the tub's white side.

Sweet Boy, call me Angel. Watch me rise.

My levitating breasts would break the bath's
Salt skin.)

        The candle fire exhaled, the fan
Kicked on. The crossbills nesting in the duct
Dueted semibreves.

        (Here, in our poem
They'd be Sirens singing *Eve, O Eve, O Eve's*

A whore because all epics need a villain,
And, Boy, I'd hope to fall. But still, I'd float
As funneled water danced around the plug.

And *O* the epigraph would toy with *Man's*
First disappointment, this one mine, the world
Without music.)

               I listened hard and heard
Just splashes when you left the room for bed.

I stayed behind, the Naked Bard, all wet
In an empty tub, the Temptress, dear, without
Device, without allure, without you here.

White Dwarf

Story goes, I came sallow:
Sister All High Yellow, a mass
Of bister skin, Miss Bonnie Lass,
Smooth, brown, and soft as mallow

Cremes – five pounds of "Ten" –
And staged, the story goes, to star.
A peek inside my repertoire?
Ladies and Gentlemen,

I bawled a loud lament.
I harmonized with the squealing cart
And nurse's *shh* – the doctor's chart
Aflap – so discontent

They tagged me twice: birth name
And Drama Queen. I've played a Cow,
Diana Ross, Wise Man and (*ow!*)
La Sexpot (conquered, I came)

In Jezebel-high fishnets.
Fingers flying on Steinway black,
I waltzed Chopin's three-quarter track
In *forte*, and duets

For one in Bach's inventions.
I do the hypochondriac.
I star depressed and zodiac-
Affected, all dimensions.

When the sun sets low and the moon
Sits high, stars constellate. And if
I'm one of them, like a hieroglyph,
Celestial cartoon,

Then call me Scorpio,
Ruler of death, rebirth. (Look, Mom,
I've left the earth.) Like a homemade bomb,
Exhausted stars die slow

To fireless gas with no
Tint or explosion, just a black hole.
And here in bed, all rock 'n' roll
Celebrity with no

Time for the little people,
I smile for the camera phone.
Fuck star and stage. Fuck microphone.
And I'll still sing as I steeple

Chase-me across the room,
Busy Girl, White Dwarf, the one who stole
The chameleonesque yet gene-fixed role
Auditioned in the womb.

Chocolate Thunder

I was born, Mom says, dancer-
Physiqued, lean leg and arm, or, hand
For five down low, born *You the Man*ned,
*Go Girl*ed, and Dad's wrong *Answer*

To dead ball dreams. I tore
Shit up, handled the no-look pass
And a jig. Somebody smack my ass.
Now who's your daddy? Score.

Darryl Dawkins wrote a book,
And I might too. He liked the rhymes'
(*If you ain't groovin'*) paradigms
(*You best get movin'*). Hook

A chorus and we've got
A song, a stereo type, a *lieu*
De mémoire with a residue
Of minstrelsy: a forgot-

Me-not like an earworm, like
The scar telling a Frankenstein-
esque tale on Dad's left heel, like fine
Fixed fantasies. They psych

Us to the frame of mind
Where we were great once too. And if
My mind were framed, like a logogriph
With images, I signed

And, baby, I went pro!
Black Bird flew high; and there's Magic and Rick
In memory's new rhetoric
If I remember 'fro,

Chocolate Thunder

Think Jordan moves, and how
The crazies love the Nappyhead
Queen James: *Goddamn she's talented*
And black in the headlines now.

High Heel

I was born, Mom says, bull's eye
Parfait, without a flaw – reflex
And one repro of fine she-sex –
All lash and rock-a-bye-

Full lids looking to close,
Slim collarbone, and rosebud pout,
I'm Queen Without a Doubt
Of all hatched embryos.

Long may I reign with a spine
Perfected in its curvature's
Half curlicue and constant manicures
On two flat feet. I line

My ankles up and, see,
They propinquate. They roll until
They collapse. The missing insteps spill
From the slingbacks' nudity

And barest ties. So call
Me Mary Jane with a turf toe fetish.
I'm stacked. With three-inch-high coquettish
Stilettos, I'm Belle o' the Ball

And socket joint. *There goes
High Heel*. I've heard my ankles crack
And traced the point where I go black
To white on all ten toes

(Top brown to bottom peach)
As if my foot's biracial. In
The lady's pump, I'm genuine
Sunday Best (Praise Jesus! Preach!*)*.

I'm the club's platforms. And though
I'll never arabesque *en pointe*,
I stand, bipodal, to disappoint
With all this bod, dance the foe

's faux *pas de deux* with the full-
Length mirror. I'm patent, polished, buffed,
Strap-bound, and muled. I'm powderpuffed.
I'm pinched. With a push and pull,

I make my blisters pop
In a serous ooze. If I could name
The foot's small bones, I'd play a game
And count the talus, cop

The dice and cuneiform,
The mid-foot characters (the wedges
Somewhere beneath the thong's thin edges),
The cuboid, and linguiform

Long toes in dual tones.
My skeleton is narratory,
Completely born and half a story
Writ large in genes and bones.

Rikki-Tikki-Tavi

And still, I'm *Tica Toc*
Or *Tikki Tavi*, tactile tongue
Twister (for Mom), forever young,
Born pitched to jabberwock

Like a pixie myth or a book's
Story in pictures (Rikki's fight,
Bright cobra's hood). I'm born to write
Myself a gerenuk's

Long leg and slender neck.
But no. I'd make me Jungle: over-
Grown in scallions, mint, sweet clover,
Lyriope deep in our deck

And all its slatted shadows,
Slim willow limbs like straightened hairs
Of angels, black, from constant stares
At the sun and superimposed

Nimbi. I wouldn't say
A word. I couldn't, as a plant.
So as I live and breathe…And can't
You see it, Piaget:

To operate, concrete,
Hushed as a sidewalk flower bed?
There's an opening there, and there you spread,
Pretty in your conceit.

II

Pianist Pretending Chopin

I amaze myself, or at least I've caught my eye
Or hands, and the cuticles' half moons. And then,
In mirrored Steinway black, they multiply,
Ten out, ten in, two hitting A, again,
Again, dampered in *one-two-three*. The den-
like room, the lasting chords, are fit for the *danse*,
The *valse*, and aristocracy. I glance

At the minor triad, reach, and take a chance.
I close my eyes with my preponderance
To the shiny veneer, Landino-blind. And when
I lose my spot to girls with cyclamen
Tucked tight behind their ears, they fly. They fly.
I fall. They fly. They whirl around with men.
I pretend the chord won't fade away and die.

Weathercock

from Granddad's Wake, Christ's Church, Oakland Mills Road

Weathercock not in the sense of weather, cock,
Or a hybrid combination of the two,
But rather in the sense of an overstock
Of sense. Here, I emote as I go through
The motions, nod and smile from the pew,
And move too much, and see too much. He's called
Frank, saint, good soul. His shiny face is bald

Except for a patch beneath his chin. He's dolled-
Up in his holy cloth. And when Dad bawled,
I thought too much and watched the mourners throw
Perfection on the dead like residue,
Like spit-shine. Life turns nursery rhyme: the stock
Old tales and *girl, remember when?* I do.
With chiseled epitaphs and dated rock.

And rocking back and forth, I go along.
The sun lowers itself in the stained-glass pane
And Aunt Bob sings the Lord's Prayer into song.
I slump on the white oak's pew and trace the grain,
The quartersawn wood's waves. Despite my vain
Attempts at grief, I only cry when a hair
Blows in my eye, and, down the thoroughfare

The casket, lily-topped, his pied-à-terre,
Goes on the shaky gurney's cockle stair,
Lattices at either side of its funeral train
Like a pair of double helices. In plain
Silence, I think of nothing. But the aisle's long
And the congregation's mute. I wear the stain
Of a dark blue leaded sun, its shine too strong.

When the City Calls Me Names

I holler back, and the whore on spikes –
You know you want it – knows, and all
The houses in the skyline's dykes
Sit there, despondent, and the scrawl

Of dawn that doesn't wake with fall-
ing stars and coal-dark skies still burns.
And the harbor speaks. And shadows crawl.
And though the harbor's big lip turns

Downward with the dock's hard U, returned
From the clouds, Orion shows as one
Big smile, but no one stops concerned
When the whore calls out, *You don't want none?*

And *nigger bitch* blares like a gun
Misfired right on target, wide
But tight. Let me hold it, load it, run.
Eels ride the slick. Night's quick on the tide.

If you died today and were reincarnated,
what would you be?

Not me, Sweet Boy, but a body with the breasts
Of Fun Time Skipper and those take-me lips
On wailing babies; unloosed hair, the tips
Tickling collarbones until it rests
Between the blades; pink gums; big teeth; the West's
Blue eyes so lunar, round as the post-eclipse
Man in the moon, but better, whiter; hips
For days like an hourglass that stands the tests
Of memory – the ingénue in chi-
Chi golden flecks on silver screens where, matte
In 40s black and white, the pin-curled Rita
Hayworth smiles. I read somewhere that she
Was half Latina. I'd come back as that.

Sweet Boy, you'd have me spotted like a cheetah.

Pianist "Clair de Lune"

Even the night has its clarity.
– Wendell Berry

(Andante)

It knows something I don't: the metronome
Ticking its silent count. I match its blows
And voice *One*
        and a Two. Lit by the gloam
Outside, I hurry
        Three as if it knows
How everything unfolds. Then the note goes,

(Un poco mosso)

And the una corda shifts the shaky ground
The keyboard's on and damps the D-flat, wound

Down low where the strings are pulled and hammers pound.
The moon is the night's own counted moves, half round

(Animato)

Like grace notes, gone and sustained in vertigos
Of a snow-collapsing sky, the crystals pose
As a bowler perched atop the streetlamp's dome.
And a One and a Two and a Three, lights presuppose

(Calmato)

Clarity or dizziness in monochrome.

Brown Recluse
from the basement

Talking in bed ought to be easiest
– Philip Larkin

But it's talking to yourself – inside, as cars
Pass by, high beams like April lightning, mist
On your slat windows bending beams to bars
Broken – and only you, no accompanist
But the fiddleback over a game of whist,
Bid whist, big joker up. You're the champion
Trickster, playing all the roles. The skeleton

Of a spider's web, in fragile strands, breaks, spun
By the roving fan, picking up carrion
Crickets, cat-mangled flies that seemed to twist
Into hysterics when the light bulb hissed
Itself to death. The glass bruises. The char's
Spreading. It's black. And, damn it, you do exist
Beneath the ceiling's darkened stucco stars,

Or sea anemone, or coral reef
In an inverted ocean where the sun
Would pierce your body or the crumpled sheaf
Of dog-pissed papers, berber threads. There's none
Unless you see it, say it, Darlin' Hon.
You lie as if dead-starfish fucked, and kissed,
Legs spread, arms out. You're your clandestine tryst

Ménage a un. You write yourself a list
On Post-it notes rustling in one tightened fist
Then tossed aside. You're subterranean
In your own words. You're Machiavellian.
You're fine, big-voiced and mum, verbose and brief.
Rain swells in flooded corners, stains near one
Sole on its side with a clinging maple leaf.

Bees in the Attic

When to the sessions of sweet silent thought
I summon up remembrance of things past
– William Shakespeare

As if I'd move enough to make a noise
As loud as theirs, those bees, I circled around
My whirring bedroom, hurdling children's toys.
I thought my lungs would buzz the attic's sound,

Crescendo, *shh* and hum; went round until
I lost my breath, lay down. The ceiling wet,
White dark with the hive, I dreamt the comb would spill
Its honey on my pink blankets. When it met

My lips the plaster lath would crack, and sweet
Dead bees stuck to the stucco shards would swarm
My face. I'd drown in wings and the petite
Menagerie with the giant verve. So, warm

And wrapped, I moved the covers, stood on my toes
And reached, and to this day nobody knows

I reached. And to this day nobody knows
The stucco's crimson dot came from my tongue.
When helping Mom in our small kitchen, I flung
The spinach-water and the afterflows

Of faucet-drips with flicking fingers, throws
To the fogged window above the sink. They clung,
I waited, for seconds until the window wrung
Itself of green, steam tears and the glass sang the woes

Of hissing chicken thighs fried in the cast
Iron pot. And the window sang in Grandma's voice,
"Go Down, Moses," and the stained-glass sugar plum

Fairy that hung on the liquid pane at the last
"My people go," raised up her hands. "Rejoice!"
I heard the bees from there growl in a hum.

From there, I heard the bees growl in a hum
Everywhere, in Sylvan lilacs that I picked
For the basement's dollhouse, singing in the drum-
ming dryer's pulse as the washer flowed and clicked.

Their noise was huge to the pint-sized figurines
Who had no ears, but eye-shaped mouths. I posed
Their arms and legs in small domestic scenes
Of "Daddy's home," their tiny red door closed,

Their eye-mouths always open in a gasp
Or scream, as if something were about to fall
Upon their house like the locust plague. The hasp
Was fastened tight. I knocked them down, played all

Four died before the darkness could descend
As if, somehow, I'd write their perfect end.

As if somehow I'd write the perfect end
To every moment, tonight, outside my house
Long left behind, I watch a hydrant douse
A child. And when I let the darkness bend

Around me in a blink, I fade to black.
Eyes closed, I eulogize the Harbor's dock,
Old Bay, the lit-up Bromo-Seltzer clock
Blue in the smoke from the beacon, the factory stack,

Night's quasi-black against the smoke's bright white.
The voice inside my head is talking smack.
The coda of today is just tonight,
No climax, only here and the bric-a-brac

Of memories just fond in retrospect.
In them, the spring's azaleas genuflect.

In them, that spring, azaleas genuflect,
Wilting, about to die in our little garden;
The noon sun bores too hot; sweat droplets harden
And case my cheeks as new weeds bottleneck

The ants in sidewalk cracks. That spring, I cried
And checked and checked in mania. I died
My hardest but it never took. No doubt
I didn't have the guts to try. But I'd scout

Locations (tool shed? shower? tub?), and Dad
And Mom, in separate rooms, would sleep right through
My tiptoed wandering about our blue,
Big siding house. I settled on the plaid

Of my own sheets, penning the letter in
My head. It pounded with adrenaline…

It pounds in my head with my adrenaline.
Dear Mom,
            Call me the dummy, the mannequin,
Dead as the dancer in the box that sings
The Mendelssohn on the top shelf and rings
With the scope of bells, and vibrates with the sound

Of clocks. The clock ticks loud as Fall rewound
At every equinox, again and again.

And when you think of me remember when
I last said Sorry. As the autumns pass
At quarter to five, the time goes fast, and the grass
Will slow its growth. But I am huge in your head,
Pounding. And we're the same. Your blood I've bled.
You're sleeping in my bed now with my bees.
I'm swimming in the hollow sound of seas.

And now I'm swimming in that sound of seas,
The inexhaustible murmur. Now I'm back
To letters at this desk of letters, keys,
Paper and screen, your egomaniac,

Dear critics. The narcissist's tried "art" inside
This paper's looking-glass, distorted, wide
With me and my burned hair, a blistered ember
From the core of the stove's hot comb. And I remember

My silence sweet as canopy beds or a girl
In spinning duchess satin's whispered whirl.
Then, all the days ahead were bees in the attic,
The moments still unseen but heard, ecstatic,

Promising blood as I stood, now stand, all poise,
As if I'll move enough to make a noise.

III

Disorder

For some diagnoses, the appropriate code depends on further specification.
– American Psychiatric Association

I'm systematically deranged.
Two. Nine. Six. Three. I've multiplied
The digits, switched, then disarranged
The code, prognoses side by side.
And I begin. I'm certified,
Depressed, no symptoms to decode.
The signifier signified
In this recurring episode.

And then the code is rearranged –
Two. Nine. Six. O, a manic ride.
It's me, sleeping all day exchanged
For vacuuming, a Flo Jo stride.
With spasms, ticks, I'm bona fide
Fucked up, bipolar antipode
And looking at the small divide
In this recurring episode.

But wait, the code is interchanged –
Two. Six. Three. I can step outside
Myself and leave me there, estranged.
Delirium's like suicide
Without the mess, more dignified.
Now bury me in my abode
Twelve feet under. Pretend I've died
In this recurring episode.

Yet I wake up, always inside
This room, writing the palinode –
Two. Nine. Six. Three – identified
In this recurring episode.

Episode

I'm the main character, played grandiose
Between two choric songs of tragedy,
And broadcast live, from *epeisodios*
(A coming in between) to synecdoche
(A part becoming an identity),
Without a thought. When everything's gone numb,
Body and mind, *Figuris terminum,*

I blank and think Descartes: *I think I* (um…)
And therefore think it's just a fantasy,
Digression, incident, *ad nauseam,*
The femme fatale's drug-fucked-up legacy,
Dark, episodic, done. And there I'll be,
Until to the grand stage I say *adios,*
Bit player, tall and lanky, lachrymose.

OCD

The learned men call it all a true
Emergency, the summer's long,
Tireless drought. And I walk through
The public park breaking the thong
Of my flat flip flop, limping in strong,
Gross heat while the proletariat
Of honey-suckle wilts along.
Quod me nutrit me destruit.

When Death strolls past, what will they do,
The pussy-willows in the throng
Of goldenrod turned brown, but cue
The organ, its sepulchral song
In desiccating sun, grow long
And tall in soil, fertile, fit?
The bell will toll – one loud ding-dong.
Quod me nutrit me destruit.

Deep in the trees, two schoolboys chew
On grass and toss their homemade bong
Inside a bag when I step through
The bush. The smell of smoke is strong.
They stay with me, wading the long
Path of the littered rivulet.
Without a clue, they nod along.
Quod me nutrit me destruit.

I always know where I belong.
Lock all the gates. I'm desperate
To hear birds sing my constant song,
Quod me nutrit me destruit.

Portrait of the Artist Musing as Speaker

I

Another I, they'll think it's you. And that's
Simple logistics. Call me the cast, the catch,
The line. I wrote "the fucking masterpiece
Of bathroom sex" for an assignment once
And said *I'm not myself tomorrow*. My,
The smell of Scrubbing Bubbles™ made me nauseous.

II

At the National Zoo, I watched a big Great Ape
Ape tamarins who were aping me. We penned
A dirty limerick. *For Blumenbach –*
There once was a girl who felt that she was closer
To apes than other men who'd kissed her neck,
And thought, Man, those bonobos must be jealous.

III

The eyes themselves are mimicry. One moves,
The other follows suit. You close the Left,
It traces open Right, trundled beneath
The lid like a lymph node, a ball in the flesh,
A ball on the bone. And still I see the light.
Oh, right. *I've seen the light*. I'm living. Yay.

IV

I like the graveyard *more*. Shadows from a plane
Pilot through pansies and the sky is earth,

Vice versa, and the marbled headstones clouds.
Sunflower stems curl round as suns and rise
Up, lively, with the moon. In the stiff, stale heat,
I like to think they're also dying soon.

V

There's hardly distance in the speed of sound
From my own mouth – just time, derivatives,
Vanishingly minute. I'm no man's bard
And portraiture will hardly change. There's age.
There's laurelled image, glare, and vanity.
My anadem is only this dark hair.

Portrait of the Artist Drawing Artist Portraits

Dionysian: ecstatic, orgiastic, undisciplined; in the philosophy of Nietzsche,
of creative-intuitive power as opposed to critical-rational power

I make them disappear, brain stem,
Right hemisphere and left ... *pro tem*,
    Two plain old figurines, no ear,
    Heads hollow but for eyes, arms sheer
To bodies straight as crosses – then hem,

Triangle skirts, big diadem
And dandelion blowball gem.
    My artists fly the atmosphere.
      I make them. Disappear,

Stick girls. Heads in the clouds. Contemn.
Or, if you want, an apothegm:
    Run cock-eyed naked twat right here
    Like hopped-up banshees. The sun is clear
And doubled. When I stare at them
    I make them disappear.

I make them disappear? My femme
Artistes, so sad and hardly femme
(Or, really, critically French, austere
    Or diacritical, no tear
Honest to Byron, Chaucer's "wem")

Are Dionysian *ad hominem*.
I draw them lying down. *Ad rem*,
    I pen that as a lavaliere.
      I make the "m" disappear

On their necks, and rewrite *read*. For them
Lying's standing. To their arms, I stem

Penciled fingers, to their bodies, a smear
Of lipstick. Red, they're dyed severe
In paper grave and apothem.
I make them disappear.

Exam Room Three

If I could be nineteen again…
At twenty-two you're dead.

I heard that notion in my head,
Sitting in the orange chair and flipping through
A *Woman's Day* from 1996. A stocky nurse
Appeared. She led me to
Exam Room Three and showed me where to lay my purse.
The room was warm. My face was red.
I got undressed.

Biting my lower lip, I tried
To hold back tears. The needle poked, slid in
My breast. The paper gown tucked underneath my arm made a crink-
ling noise. I flinched. My skin
Burned as he eased it out, then in again. "I think
The odds are clearly on our side,"
The doctor stressed.

A week was packed in every day,
Or so it seemed, waiting. I can't think back
To how it felt. I think of how it was, the way the light
Bulb died, the useless stack
Of magazines I bought to fill the time, the night
He called, the word "benign." I play
A game and test

Myself, again. I picture me,
A gurney in a sterile room the day
I finally die: the masks, the I-V drugs, cold, slow inside
My veins, the chills, the way
The disinfectant lingers there. And fear? I hide
From that. I give myself a C.
Average. At best.

Anatomy

I   In the lab

A fetus inside a large cross section
Of a womb, like two dead lying lovers
Asleep inside a liquid tomb,
A child and faceless mother spoon,
Painted topaz.
            Light warms the cold,
Restores the sight to those who watch
From jars near bovine skulls.
                     Mid-nod,
Amphibians float peacefully.
I fall behind. The tour moves on
Through gifts of God, and every one
Is perfect, masterly preserved,
Opened, sleeping, eyes wide, and dumb.

II   On the table

Ladylike, I'm *born this way*,
(*And fine*) she says
                 without a face.
I only see the ceiling when
She feels my uterus tip toward
My spine. *Retroverted.* So I
Imagine it:
           When the organ tilts
Backwards, it fractures bone. Chips tear
Through skin and lingerie wet with the stain
Of washed-out blood.
              It falls between
The tile's white grid, rubber-tipped doorstops,
Attached fallopian tubes like small

Eight-fingered hands on ovaries.
If the grip goes loose, they'll spin like tops.

III   In the mirror

I have my mother's face, though I,
Hair perfect in the comb, just made up
My face with cotton swabs and shadows.
My big fee fi faux grin glows even
In the flicker of vanity lights.
                        Sweet ass,
I'll take you home. And I will carry
My organs as accessories.

Dressed up, I'll tuck my uterus
Beneath my arm. For warmth, I'll sling
The stretched fallopian tubes across
My shoulders, left side off a bit
To show some skin. I'll do the town,
Come back and sleep alone curled up
Beneath the crimson back-lit moon's
Night-light
                not yet ballooning full
From February's crescent stage.

Placebo

I've become the remedies –
Two pills, Crown Royal and water
Bittersweet with roses, the Daughter
Of Fine Absurdities.
I am the antiphon.
And I'm responding for the dead
In mind on mornings when the head
Does acrobatics on
The clouds. I'm naked in
A stranger's home, twelve needles placed
Like hairs in living tissue, spaced
On each meridian,
Black Voodoo Doll, all doubt
In the open, and now I've bet
The whole fake farm. The table's set.
And I breathe in, breathe out,
Hearing hushed new age music
On empty limestone patios.
I am the Great Placebo,
The great placebo, sick
In the same old waiting room.
I am the lab where everything
Does what it doesn't do. Getting
Well, I see the concrete bloom,
And I find happiness
In leaves soaking like wrinkled hands
In tepid baths of rain, frail hands
I hope to slap then kiss
Until the dithyramb
Fades to a headache, though I am too
Far gone to flinch and nothing's true.

I don't know what I am.

IV

Credo

As a woman, I have learned
Some men are really bad

At whispering, as if
Their tenors can't be tempered,

Slight winds, perhaps, more apt
At fine seduction. Still,

Give me their manly lows,
The broader pitch of *Os*,

Pharynx tremors, and hard
Gs. Now I've come to think

Their throats are coated red,
Bright red, engorged, a sinew

Of veins across their necks
When they inflect a sound

And swallow, understood.
Though something should be said

For breath, an *h* unseen
In *God*, lipped in *Come here*,

My mouth is big. I think
I'm ready for my manhood.

Busy Man

If Busy Man wears many hats
Then someone get me one big ol'
Sombrero – just one job, the cat's
Big dog meow to one who stole
The gist but never skimmed the whole
Dang self-help book in Border's half-
Off section,
                    novice, like a calf
Stumbling to its knees when I go down
Like a heifer, hoarding crap to put
Beneath my tongue: threads from brown
Carpet or the wide-ruled notepad's foot
Of poetry – all work – and soot –
And play – picked off a match after I bate
My breath and blow and so regurgitate
My breath as smoke.
                         The more I eat
The more I grab, and gorge, until
On Monday Dr. Misconceit
Plates up a dose of Seroquel –
Just one. You take JUST ONE. – for *ill-*
Fated but *No…no…NOT…psychotic….*
(Sweet Boy and I prefer *exotic*.)
He says, *My god, you're done for. Sleep.*

I listen, but, in threes, I hear
The Nutcracker's last bars, the creep
To the end as Gelsey Kirkland's sheer
Nightgown slowly sways and the queer
Phrasing spins eddies spun not fast
Enough. (For parallax … at last
It's done.) *Say what*, i.e., *what God?*
I ask.

Well, He don't sleep. He's at
His padlocked gates, laid back with an odd
Expression and his trilby hat
Cocked low. He winks, and I know that,
That, God, that God ...THAT God still waits
For Sunday's off and recreates
Since God must go a little crazy,
Too, when the night skies in between
Columbus and here don't appear as hazy
Or dark, but bleed like a knifed-up scene,
Like bludgeon rust and swaddling, clean
White gauze.
                    He's up and at it again.
He needs a piss, another pen
For names, more names, just one last name
In His book. His wrinkled hand is cramped
To a claw or shaped in a hellish flame,
Or teardrop, yes, the one that damps
The spark when, back at work, my lamp's
Burned out and I strike strike strike the thin
Long match and scorch my chin
To taste the smell of my own skin –

Press on, Busy Man. Press on. Chew through
Your cheek and do it right, your grin
Like hunted hides, drenched in its true
Colors. Grind down to the bone; gnash; spew
Supper, and search high and low for your halo and penance
And a murder of crows and your birthday's sentence.

Somewhere Between Columbus and Cincinnati

If you die today, where will you spend eternity?

Jesus, it's a stretch of few

And far between the repetitions: fenced-
In fields and Christ's billboard-dispensed
       Commandments. There **HELL IS REAL**
       Worn in the corners, peel-

ing like dead skins (**McRIB** beneath).
Fence posts decay like rotting teeth.
       Sun spreads dusk's morning *deux*.
       Pale pink eclipses blue

And it's all memorial, two brown
Bottles, the worms a wren will down.
       The shattered ambers burn.
       And if the salmon cloudlets turn

Pitch-black, I will believe in You.

That Time Frank Thought a Plastic Bag was a Jellyfish

for my brother

Fish carcasses were crowding me,
Or so I claimed as I pretended, froze,
Feet in a bed
Of skeletons when a free
Floating Sprite bottle feigned a dolphin's nose.
Driftwood was hammerhead;
Dunes, cleft

Palates in the harbor's mouth. *So you're
A smartass*, he said. I said I felt the sting,
Salt in nicked calves,
And knew we could be sure
A dollar wasn't seaweed, severed string
Not fish shit. Sea in halves,
Quick, deft,

Broken, the waves would rise and fall.
Out past the break, we sensed no moves. Frank saw
The sun set like
It used to when we'd call
Reflections gold – *It's mine. No mine* – and the awe
Of the thing was the diving pike
And heft

Of skipped stones as they broke a brook.
Did I see? Carcass was stone, stone shells, maybe
An avatar
Of bodies, the sands mistook
For dirt. We drifted, the shore like an effigy.
Right where we were was far
From left.

Semantics

Right now I much prefer
Darkie in place of African-
American – the melanin
More obvious. As per
Political Correct-
Ness, wait, I'll reconsider Black:
Reflecting little light, a lack
Of predominant hue – effect:
Very dark.

*

This black, Mom said,
Was born when an up-north matriarch
Got hitched back in the day, went dark
In Texas. Brillo head
Met roller hair, a lean
And knobby knee wearing a layer
Of darker skin. Our jaws curve square
And round, some aubergine
("Blue black"), some fair. Some who?
Darkies. Remember? I'm in question.
So when a man asked (with suggestion?),

*

"You got Indian in you?"

*

I told him Black and yes.
Characterized by cheerless sullenness,
No light, pictured in an evening dress,
I smile, incandesce,

And flash. My teeth are white.
The rest is shadow.

*

Perceptions of
Black appear to depend (above)
On the contrast with bright
And colored stimuli.
Black: zero stimulation to
The retina.

*

A vision too
Invisible? I try
To block the light, eyes closed,
But I'm at perihelion.
Even the Tiffany lamp's a sun
And I am too exposed.

*

Some days I just see red.

*

Outside, twisting like ivy stems,
My black is brown as periblems
And the empty flowerbed

Collecting rain. Is sheen
More relevant, more true, than hue?

And do I shine? This jigaboo
Moves here in shades of green.

Motherland

I'm wearing Africa
On my brown stomach: a birthmark
Dotted with freckles, nevus dark
And ticklish. *Laugh 'Rica,*

Mom says. *The master stoles*
Himself a spotty people. I see
A darker reef and symmetry
In her black island moles.

*

And Dad? With hazel eyes,
Lightskin-ded peach, 'fro in the shears,
He was pretty as mums and rabbits' ears.
I thought he was white. Then, the skies

Wore their own cicatrix
In blackberry winters, dark and light,
Bright orange and blue. A lightning sprite
Ignited willow sticks.

*

In the August heat, I start
To sweat behind my ears, beside
Keyloids and studs. The droplets slide.
They're warm as blood. They dart

From jaw to collarbone,
My breast, I think, still sometimes bleeds.
I bandage up scar tissue beads
I scour with pumice stone.

*

When the nipple's hard and cold,
The areola raises the line
The scalpel left before *Benign*.
Now, like a centerfold,

I cup it with my palm.
The staples' zippered prints, like pins
In silk, remain. The wrinkle thins
To flat and fleshy calm –

*

If skin is ever calm
With nerves and veins. Though clean,
The flesh has bugs. By the window's screen,
I rub my arms with balm

And watch the insects flit
And polka dot my pink chemise.
So, shadowpox me, flies. Disease.
The tiny stains could fit

*

Between my legs. The skin,
So dark, looks purple as a bruise.
I find a new mole to amuse
My fear of cashing in.

I scrape the spot and sweep
It aside – small clots, perhaps, where I'd

Made me a child that might've died
Unnoticed in my sleep.

Face in the Pillow

Then I can't say a word,
Or rather, no, he can't discern
The words I'm saying, only learn
The muscles mute and heard

In mimicry of boy
And girl. Hips twitch. The calves say *Faster*.
The back cracks, *Say my name*. *Master*.
Mistress. As cunt turned toy,

I quiet down, and dark
Makes off with the pillow. It numbs
Until, like steps in snow, he comes
And I have left my mark.

In Consonance with the Order of Things

during the NCAA tournament, 1993-2006

Billy Packer's starting to piss me off,
The constant chatter: *Agh! Tying free throw's off
The iron ... Dreams dead at the stripe ... now off
To Greg back in the studio.* He's off
And running with new favorites. Fickle. New off-
Guard's *good* (wait) *bad*. The *nickle-dimers ... off*

The hooks – I'm black and I can't pull that off.
So where's my book? My Freud? Case II. He's off
Cold-casing old obsessed neurotics off
Their rockers, off their medications, off
In Oedipus land ... Was I dozing off?
That's weak. Psychotic Dr. Schreber's off

To the sanitarium. He says he's off
Marrying God. Next page the wedding's off.
Case III. Freud thinks some shit and then gets off.
꙳

A futile miss. To Do?: Think thoughts; piss off
The doctors; drink; drink more. Time's ticking off
The clock. Ball's out of bounds. Billy says off

A foot, and Freud would take the gym shorts off
And make the zone erogenous, spin off
The *picks* to *I love dick* like it's water off
A duck's back. To Do?: Get fucked. Go fucking off.
Warble a fight song near the key of F
Since, fucking A, cacophony's an off-

Shoot. Hey, I might just win, knock the glass right off
The chandelier and chant a clear, *Get off
It, fuckface.* There's me in team. So deemed, I'm off –
Hot down the stretch. To Do?: *Ta-da*. Shoot off

Your middle, ring, and pinkie threes. Close off
The O. Now scream. Time sticks and then ticks off.

A season lost? Three zeroes triple off
From 7, 6 ... So maybe something's off
And maybe this is heaven. Days peel off
The calendar, the *shining moments*, off
And trashed. Where are you, Billy? Off
Air? Smashed? I'm one on one. The TV's off.

Banners have waved and horns have sounded off.
My team's gone down, and I've been carried off.
I bleed and heal. And rip the scabs right off.

The Platitudinous and the Clever

At parties always seem to know
      Just what is what
And what to say: *That Fresca's no*
      Martini; But

For nothing none is nearly one.
      The shaved white poodle
Barks at the chandelier's beamed sun
      And its stars canoodle

The moon in the french doors' panes. And in
      The room, on the wall-
Paper, plum grapes and muscadine,
      A mirror, astral,

Hangs from a hook, and the glass is filled
      With my own face.
The frame shows lovely gold and gild-
      The-lily. Lace

Garlands surround the crackling edge.
      Without it, it
Could be a window, sortilege
      Even. I sit

Both in the dining room and out,
      Breathy in fog,
The deck's pipe smoke, wispy but stout,
      Lingering. The dog

Stops barking as I start to mouth
      Sounds from the speakers,
Barely singing lyrics, my mouth
      Open, weak; hers

Big, I'd imagine, as she sings
      The aria.
I steal her "Un Bel Di," the strings,
      Pensive, for *uh…*

Uh… um, and stand her shore, alike
      Near colliers, fish
And chum. My God, I smell the pike.
      There's blood. I wish

Her title were my axiom.
      In that moment
I'm her succor. *Sucker?* I'm dumb.
      It's testament

To parallax. It's parable
      For solitude.
When everything is errable,
      Vicissitude

Goes wild. All opposites are the same
      And extensions
Of one. Oh. That's a clever game.
      Trite attention's

Lost its luster. Here comes the cake
      And all the while
Puccini playing by mistake.
      And on the tile

My highball cracks. Clear liquor settles
      Inside the grooves
And grout. The sound sounds too much metal's
      Metallic; moves

Like singlet streams swimming to touch –
    They don't – an ooze
Like blood between bodies that clutch
    But never bruise.

That Time Frank Thought about the Tree of Life

I saw the tree that broke,
Fell fast. We didn't see
It coming, heard no crack,
That proverbially yelled, *Timber!*
Or even its loud timbre.
We heard the tires squeal.
We only saw its end
Like a pendulum stopped half-
Way through its traced half circle.
We saw it slow, saw burn
Behind our wheels, wet bract
Toward the median.
When Black-eyed Susans kicked
High in the air, it split.
Gold petals rose like smoke.

And yet, before it sprung
Uprooted, in the ground,
What did the rot look like?
If I held an ear to an oak
Could I hear it? The tree,
Perennial, would sound
Like death, echo like shells,
Smell of unscented baths,
And depress like sponges. If
I were there to see, I'd drink
Its water and it'd fall
Without a sound. And if
It had a taste, it'd taste
Of swallowed medicine
Left sour on the tongue.

Parallax

Icicles plummet from the porch and sow
Drips, prisms, rainbows, daggers celestial
In their own right. They're lit with touch-and-go
Low beams. The moon slices residual
Storm clouds. Kaleidoscopes, the crystals crack
Colorless on the concrete and land in black.
You stare that black *more* black until the three
Branches across the street from a broken tree
Lose edges, shape, and still the vantage – last
Before you sleep. Through hedges you can see.
The train is coming slow and coming fast.

The later it gets, the more the sky will glow
In a strange reversal. Immaterial,
The stars are hidden in the indigo
Turning to rose, pinks so prophetical
Of sunny days – our nightly almanac.
And on the quarry lake the mallards quack.
Drakes lift and soar as if they're willowy
Feathers. A squawking goose attempts to flee
Their noise. He flaps his wings in the water's blast
Of droplets rising from the ice debris.
The train is coming slow and coming fast.

The more you sleep, the harder it is to throw
The nightmare off yourself, with its optical
Illusion and your eyes closed. Then, with no
Vision, your every where is visual.
I had a soundless dream once, saw the smack
Of cedar switches, saw the sting on black
Limp bodies, like spring blooms, hanged delicately
From a bough, strange fruit, decaying canopy
Of shade. I picked each one. One laughed at me.

He mouthed, blue-lipped, *We'll fall eventually*.
The train is coming slow. And coming fast,

The wind-blown icicles and jagged snow
Knock at my door, alive, no, visceral
As scraping fingernails, and the curio
Skyline moves like a shaken snow globe full
Of glittered flakes inside their hands. *We're back.*
Now let us in. The taps won't stop. I pack
My ears with tissue. *Yeah, those drapes could be*
Your noose. You're history. Yes, you. Go free –
But no – *sputter and snap. Look on, aghast.*
Go on, and gag on your own gravity –
The train is coming slow and coming fast:

What parallax (seesawing winks, the grow,
The shrink, the aweing always temporal,
The voices, mine). I see the train tracks show
Straight as a V. The lights bear destinal,
An oversight on dirt and the growing stack
Of branches. It seems they'll never shine where the track
Meets street and the land spreads constant, flat, a free
Expanse of time and space. Consistently
The horn blows louder, clearer, breezes gassed
With fumes when the red eyes start to flash. Fuck me.
The train is coming, slow and coming. Fast ...

Swing low ... the arm comes down. Illusory,
The scene melds quick as prose and poetry,
And I take it all in, still, as a metaphrast.
Pied Piper, play that piccolo; tell me
The train is coming slow and coming fast.

Coda

Some days, what I remember still
Surprises me. Last year in late
May, the cicadas showed up shrill,
Their ceaseless organs airing *Mate,*
No, *mate with me.* They titillate
Me even now, high-pitched, in the drum-
ming crickets' moves to copulate
In the meantime. What I become

Sitting next to a windowsill,
Duvet-cocooned, isn't innate.
It's born with time, baring an ill-
Fated notion: long days will wait
Like hyacinths, then germinate
To more. Then, I'm living the sum
Of moments while I calculate
In the mean. Time, what you become

Is my perpetual motion, nil
Personified in pulses, pate,
Undulations of fever, chill.
The body makes me salivate.
I wonder, can they masturbate,
The nymph cicadas, can they hum
Interred in dirt? They hibernate.
In the meantime what I become

Are wakeful tries to imitate
Their sleep. Spring mimics menstruum.
Un-endings thrive, and still I hate
What, in the meantime, I've become.

V

DrugFace

1 Take with food

I was born, Mom says, big-eyed
And starved, ready to vindicate
My appetite and baby weight
As a Big Girl, bona fide,

Bona pétite. My lips
Were made for sucking bones, my tongue
For fingertips, and when the slung-
Low pants hung off my hips

(Or meat, Mom says) I worked
A real sashay. An edentate,
I licked the areola's plate
And bit Mom's nipple, smirked

Until she fed me more.
I ate the apple core and broke
A tooth. The days when she would yoke
My hair in plaits, I wore

A do-rag fit enough
For Aunt Jemima, Aunt Bob said,
"Now's who's your mammy, Shortening Bread?"
Dear reader, yeah, I'd stuff

Myself. I'm told that food
Is anything metabolized.
I watched, and it materialized
In delicacies.
                    They stewed,

Crickets and beetle wing
Aflutter. I brake, and they fly tonight
In the high beams and twin headlight
Refractions. The entrée sings

The dinner buzz, creates
A dizzy air of vertigos.
Big WONDERBREAD looms tall and blows
A fuse. The sign deflates

To WNDERBREAD – the O,
In hemoglobin red, dying
To dark, but not before flying
In sparks with the high-heat glow

Of a stove's eye. Although
I've closed my windows, I can smell,
In synaesthesia, the shell
Of a light bulb burning slow.

I smell like cocoa butter,
Dior, and zinfandel (white) seeping
From me as if it's in there steeping,
Making its squatter Sutter

Home at home in my wasting
Wrists, Mom says. The ironic twist?
I've grown to an apologist
With cotton mouth a-tasting

Like shit. My appetite's
Been gone. But "the shell of a man," alive
Or dead, is always true. We thrive
In bone the parasites

And rot can't take. Against
The grain, score me on the cold steel slab
Like brisket. Drain me. Pray I'll gab
With the deceased and fenced-

In in pearled gates. "Melville,
Ice down Dom Perignon and I
May take a sip. But when I spy
Brillat-Savarin I'll spill

The beans and tell him I
Am nothing." When I eat again,
I'll skip the lady's madeleine
And start with foods with my

Own body parts inside,
The kidney bean, palm heart, the sweet
Meats a la carte. With Aquavit,
I'll wash it down, mouth wide

With bitter spit and pills
Like an ad reading, *Got Suicide?*
Xanax rattles in the bag beside
Me and I aim for kills,

Road kill with bloody hide,
Bowels worming like a gastrotrich.
Let's pay attention. Fuck the sick.
Driving, I'm satisfied.

I carry a heavy load.
("Look, Ma, no – ") ("Watch it, man!") DrugFace is
A song of homeo(oh)stasis
And I'm back on the road.

II Do not drive a car or operate heavy machinery until
      you know how you will react to this drug

Who knew quick-fired road-
Runners are kin to cuckoos, rain
In single-file can hydroplane,
Geese stand up pigeon-toed?

And, damn, my heart's too loud.
I was born, Mom says, to draw a crowd,
A Wonder-kin. So if I bowed,
Cocksure and high-cock-browed,

Would someone clap and pass
With a *Semper Fi* or *Brake For Squirrels*?
Who knew rain fell in funneled whirls,
Pavement's like polished glass,

White Castle's blue? Big byte-
Sized road signs spell in tiny dash-
Like marks. They flit. They fib. They flash
WRONG WAY. And here tonight,

Though grandiose, they're not
A dream. Still big-eyed, wide awake,
(Look, Ma) my body starts to shake.
I watch my polka dot

Moles in a pell-mell dance,
My fingers gripping ten and two,
Prehensily. Mom says *virtu*,
Says Lovely, Elegance,

Says, *Girl, you're in tall cotton*
Now. DrugFace gets her Miss Daisy on.
I ride the High Street autobahn
Like I have flat forgotten

To steer. I close my eyes
And hear Mom say a prayer, *Dear Lord,*
Watch over her. Hell, Ouija board
Won't help me now. Surprise –

Who knew I'd doubly expose
With open eyes? The signal's green's
Gone red. And zoom. A trip? Bad genes?
Who writes the end? Who knows

My heart *is* loud with bass
And rain *does* fall like rewound tears
Crying up the windshield. When the gears
Hum low, I'm keeping pace

With the car ahead. No doubt
Tonight, as Housman said, to the road
All runners come. But this episode
Is mine: a whirlabout

Inside the yellow lines,
Horns trumpeting, so loud, like it's
Elysium till it remits
To fog, tears, rain ..., your standard signs.

III   Do not drink alcohol while taking this medication

Hey baby what's my sign?
OPEN's in mercury, Labatt
Blue-blooded as aristocrat
Budweiser crowns. Red wine

Is Yellowtail. The thin
Stirrers go round and multiply.
I was born, I've said before, to die
With (gasp) a familial sin,

Die Grandpa's suicide:
One shot, a bullet behind a rush
Of Johnnie Walk – . *Sweet honey, hush*,
Respect the Certified,

Mom says, the *Crazy*. Jack
And Coke? Jim Beam and Branch? Why, yes.
The corner TV lights fluoresce
A dim lit strobe. Darts whack

At cork and a man plays pin-
Ball like he's fucking the sloped machine.
Fuck yeah, I'd be the Dancing Queen,
The Girl, the Mandolin,

Maudlin and moved as I sweep
Across the peanut floor and sing
Falsetto with a flickering
Bright jukebox frame. I keep

Drawing a blank so dark
My rods must readjust to focus

On this kingdom come in *taverne locus*,
And cynosural spark

Of cigarettes. St. James
Protects our patronage – "The Great"
Or "Lesser," I don't know. I sate
Myself with gin, and names

Mean nothing. Call me still
Heredity's Sad Heroine
With the boozer gene, encephalin
Sans dopamine – a Pill

(For those less technical)
With side effects intensified.
Fuck sober. Fuck me open wide.
I'll suck the bottle, lull

Myself to sleep and wake,
Later, as an amnesiac.
That Mendel guy's a garden quack.
I toast him though, and take

Another sip for old
Acquaintance I'll forget, one for
The therapist, and three or four
For earworms in Mom's bold

Big blissful voice, the bough
Always broken. Sweet lullabies
Swear falls and don't apologize.
So, Sweet Boy, kiss me now.

IV   May cause drowsiness

And down comes Baby, now,
Though the cow has yet to jump the moon
And I rock, fast, without the tune
Of "Rockabye." Allow

Me this: no sleep, but a slump,
No haze but the blurry fix of my
Depression. Like a damselfly
At rest, I'll fold as (thump

Thump thump) my heart retards.
My head goes numb until I think
Nothing (no food or ride, no drink)
But picture birthday cards –

Big clown, bright carousel –
Signed *Mom*, by Dad, when Mom was sick
As me. There's *Love* and *Rica-Tic*.
I was born, Mom says, to tell

Tall tales, born storied song
And dance who fancies make-believe,
Scheherazade, recitative;
Says, *You remember wrong*;

Says, *Fine*. I say Daughter
Knows monkeyshine. The a.m. train
Accompanies my verse and rain
With a whistle in the water,

Far off and lonely, subdued
As a dampered note, and yet (Ta-dum!)

Like the evening's perfect requiem.
Mom, hear my gratitude.

She tells me I exude
Great Soul, and I want no reprieve,
As Shakespeare warned us sleep would thieve
Us of the magnitude

Of our own company.
This company loves misery.
And that's beatitude. That's chi,
DrugFace synecdoche;

It's equilibrium
And a little death, like apnea,
A breathless beat inside the *joie*
De vivre, or dreams in dumb

Slumber. I'll doze drug free
So I can know it all: loose joints,
My sweat-wet thighs, stiff hair in points,
And Mom in mourning. I'll be

Big-Eyed Afraid, then tasting
My tongue and teeth as my throat expands
In a squeaky gulp that never lands.
Whose breath is it I'm wasting?

I pull the covers up,
Blink fast until the night-light dances
In afterglows and second chances
And reflects inside my cup

Of water still, untouched,
And sweating in a single drop.
I pick it up like it's a prop,
A moment's weeping clutched

With a fingertip and placed
Against my eye. When the tear won't fall,
I choke and cough and start to bawl.
And if a breath erased

It all, inhaled the tears
And pushed my concave belly out,
(Look Me!) I'd lose the will to shout
And hold it in. So here's

DrugFace. My makeup smears
In two black streaks across my spit-
And salt-wet cheeks. And this is it.
I was born big-voiced, with ears

Made for my lonely din
Of Daughter's Daughter, Flesh and Bone,
And the only name I've always known.
The world's outside. I'm in.

Index of Titles and First Lines

A Note About the Author

Erica Dawson was born in Columbia, Maryland in 1979. Majoring in the Writing Seminars, she received her BA with departmental honors from Johns Hopkins University in 2001. After earning her Master of Fine Arts from Ohio State University in 2006, she moved south to the University of Cincinnati, where she is pursuing a PhD in English and Comparative Literature as the Elliston Fellow in Poetry. Her poems have appeared or are forthcoming in *Barrow Street*, *Blackbird*, *Sewanee Theological Review*, *Southwest Review*, and *Virginia Quarterly Review*. She has been awarded several fellowships and prizes, including the Academy of American Poets Prize at Ohio State University. She also took second place in the 2004 Morton Marr Poetry Prize.

A Note About the Anthony Hecht Poetry Prize

The Anthony Hecht Poetry Prize was inaugurated in 2005 and is awarded on an annual basis to the best first or second collection of poems submitted. For further information, please go to the press's website, at http://www.waywiser-press.com/hechtprize.html.

Other books from Waywiser

*Expanded UK edition